Something's Different

Something's Different

Shelley Rotner and Sheila Kelly, Ed.D.
Photographs by Shelley Rotner

The Millbrook Press   Brookfield, Connecticut

To all the families going through this difficult time — SR

For P. and A.
And to Shelley Rotner, with appreciation
and admiration for her wonderful images — SK

Library of Congress Cataloging-in-Publication Data

Rotner, Shelley.
Something's different / Shelley Rotner and Sheila Kelly :
photographs by Shelley Rotner.
p.cm.
Summary: A young boy displays a wide range of emotions
as he copes with his parents' marital problems.
ISBN 0-7613-1923-9 (lib. bdg.)
1. Parent and child – Juvenile literature. 2. Emotions in children
– Juvenile literature. [1. Parent and child. 2. Family problems.
3. Emotions.] I. Title: Something's different. II. Kelly, Sheila M. III. Title.

BF723.P25 R68 2002
2001026692

Published by The Millbrook Press, Inc.
2 Old New Milford Road
Brookfield, Connecticut 06804
www.millbrookpress.com

Designer: Tania Garcia

For as long as I can remember,
my family lived in our house.

And we always did things together.

But now, things
seem different with
Mom and Dad.

They sound mad.

I can't tell what's happening.
Is it my fault?

They tell me,
"Sometimes things
change for grown ups.
It's nothing you did.

We're working on
our problems.

We'll always love you
and take care of you."

It's scary.

I don't know
what's happening.

I try not to think about it. I do my jobs.

I play with my toys.

Then I wonder: Is there some way I could fix things?

Mom and Dad say, "No, don't worry. This is our problem, and we will take care of it."

They say that they go to talk to someone whose job is helping parents to be happy together.

They say they're not getting divorced.

Sometimes I forget about the trouble.

It feels as if nothing is different . . . It feels as if everything is the same as it used to be.

Then I remember I'm scared.
I'm mad too — very, very mad.

They should stop. It's not fair.

Mom and Dad say sometimes
they feel sad and mad too.

It's hard to wait for the troubles to clear.

One day Mom took me fishing.

Another day Dad took me to the pet store.

We still have storytime every night.

I still play with my friends.

I still take care of my dog.

And Mom and Dad still love me.

One day I fixed my wagon.

I guess children
can't fix grown-ups' problems.

How much longer
will it be like this?

It's so confusing.

Mom and Dad say,
"Just remember,
we'll always love you
and take care of you."

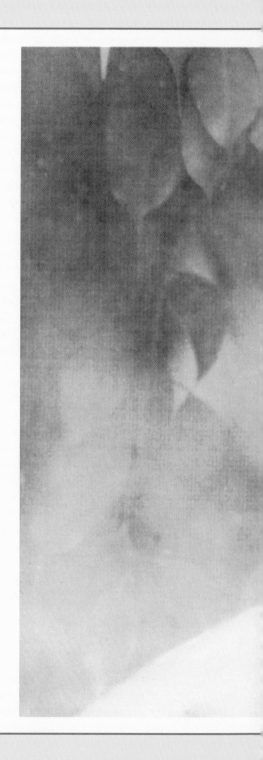

And I know they will.